i
WONDER
ABOUT
THE QUR'AN

I Wonder About the Qur'an

Published by
THE ISLAMIC FOUNDATION, 2017

Distributed by
KUBE PUBLISHING LTD
Tel +44 (01530) 249230, Fax +44 (01530) 249656
E-mail: info@kubepublishing.com
Website: www.kubepublishing.com

First published in Turkey by Uğurböceği Publications,
a Zafer Publication Group imprint, in 2008.

Text © 2008 Ozkan Oze
Translation © 2015 Selma Ayduz
Illustrations © 2008 Zafer Publishing

Author Özkan Öze
Translator Selma Aydüz
Series Editor Dr Salim Aydüz
Illustrator Sevgi İçigen
Book design Zafer Publishing & Nasir Cadir
Cover Design Fatima Jamadar

A Cataloguing-in-Publication Data record for this book is available
from the British Library

ISBN 978-0-86037-513-5
eISBN 978-0-86037-553-1

Printed by Imak Ofset, Istanbul, Turkey

BOOK

i WONDER ABOUT THE QUR'AN

Özkan Öze

Translated by Selma Aydüz

Illustrations by Sevgi İçigen

Contents

Foreword...7

Why is the Qur'an in Arabic?...13

Why should I read the Qur'an in Arabic?....................................25

Should I read the Qur'an in Arabic if I don't understand it?.............35

Why did Allah use words in the Qur'an? 43

Why was the Qur'an revealed over such a long time?.......................53

How do we know that the Qur'an has not been changed?.................61

Science in the Qur'an 73

Why does it say: "Will they not then consider the camels...?"
in the Qur'an? 83

Why is the name of the longest surah in the Qur'an
al-Baqarah (the cow)? 91

The Dictionary of the Qur'an 103

Foreword

THE STORY OF the "I Wonder About Islam" series started one day with my son asking me, "Why can't I see Allah, dad?" The question was so unexpected that I didn't know what to say, although I actually knew the answer.

But when he asked so suddenly, I just said, "Umm, well…" He opened his eyes wide and started staring at me as if to say *Come on, give me the answer!* I beat around the bush for a while. You know, I was humming and hawing. In the end, I said, "Your eyes are so small, yet Allah is so big! This is the answer to the question. Because of this, you can't see Allah!"

"Oh, really?" he said. He turned his Spider-Man toy around in his hands. Then, as if he hadn't said anything, he went to his room. He was only five years old…

Perhaps, for a child his age, this answer was enough. I had handled the situation. However, as he got older, he would ask heaps of new questions about Allah. I had to prepare my answers.

So, that is how I started the "I Wonder About Islam" series.

The best thing about this book is that not only my kids, but kids from around the world can read my answers.

The first and second books in the "I Wonder About Islam" series consist of answers I have given to questions about Allah.

In the third book, you will find answers to questions about the Prophet, peace be upon him.

The fourth book is about the Muslim holy book, the Qur'an.

Have I answered all the questions about all these topics? Of course not! I've only tried to answer the most frequently asked ones. But if you look at how I have answered these questions, it will help you work out the answers to other questions yourself. If you hang on to your question's tail and pull as hard as you can, a huge answer will follow.

And after reading this book, you will see that questions don't frighten you as much as before. You will bravely ask the questions you thought were the hardest to answer, and soon you will see that you can't think of a question that doesn't have an answer. Asking a question is saying, "I want to learn!", "I want to understand!", "I want to know better and love more!" You should never be afraid of asking questions, and don't ever give up asking questions! Because a question is a key. Every question opens a door for you. And behind every door is a whole other world.

Furthermore, asking a question is also a prayer. Make sure you pray a lot so that your mind and heart are filled with the light of knowledge; so that your path is always bright.

The "I Wonder About Islam" series has been written using the works of the great Muslim scholar Said Nursi (1878–1960). The answers given to the questions and the examples to help you understand the topics have all been taken from his *Risale-i Nur* books.

Özkan Öze
İstanbul, 2012

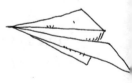

Alif Lam Mim Ra.
These are the signs of the Book.
What your Lord has sent down
to you [Prophet] is the truth,
yet most people do not believe.

Surah Al-Ra'd 13:1

Why is the Qur'an in Arabic?

We have sent it down as an Arabic Qur'an so that you may understand.

Surah Yusuf 12:2

ALIF, BA, TA are the first letters of the Arabic alphabet. This was how my first Qur'an lesson started. A long time ago.

Every summer's day, when all the children played games on the streets, I would put my Arabic book under my arm and go to the Arabic teacher's house, sad that I wasn't able to play outside.

The teacher would be waiting for me on the balcony as usual.

"Come child, come! Open up your lesson!"

The elderly woman would scan the lines of the Arabic book with me, her eyes barely visible under a pair of thick glasses.

Whenever I made a mistake while reading she was always quick to correct me. But it seemed that she never got angry or bored.

In fact, she always looked excited. Even though she had read these words thousands of times before, she happily sat there, listening to me, helping me whenever I needed it.

I didn't share her enthusiasm. Instead of looking at the Arabic letters she pointed at, I would read the bit underneath that explained how to pronounce them.

And the teacher would say: "Well done child! Well done child!" every time, and stroke my hair.

After each lesson she told my mum how well I read, how fast I learned – unaware I was cheating all along.

This went on for a month.

From time to time I would feel guilty. I was lying to that lovely old woman. However, I didn't stop.

Eventually, we finished that book – weeks before all the other children in the neighbourhood.

The teacher smiled wide and said: "Well done child, well done child! Now it is time to start reading the Qur'an!"

She gave me a copy of the Qur'an to take home. It didn't tell me, under every line, on every page, how to pronounce the Arabic.

What would I do?

The next morning I left my Arabic book on the table, put my Qur'an under my arm and started walking to the teacher's house.

Oh no! My stupid, big head! I thought all the way.

The first surah of the Qur'an is *al-Fatihah* and, thankfully, I knew it off by heart. Without making it obvious to the teacher, I hummed my way through it, and finished my lesson for the day.

The next day we started Surah *al-Baqarah*.

"Read my child… don't be shy."

"Alif Lam Mim."

Ah! This bit was easy…

"Well done child, well done!"

"Dhalika al…"

"Read child, read, don't get nervous!"

"Dhalika al-kitabuuuuuuu…"

"You were reading so well the other day… *subhanallah* what has happened?"

I struggled on for another week, the teacher reading far more than me.

Then school started, so I could breathe a sigh of relief; the lessons had come to an end.

Many years have passed since then. And I've learned that I wasn't deceiving the teacher in those lessons, I was deceiving myself.

When I was older, I had to get another Arabic book and learn to read the Qur'an by myself, at night, secretly. Each time I got stuck, I thought about my old teacher; how excited she was whenever she opened the Qur'an, how it brought her so much joy.

This is the lesson she left me with: it is a book to enjoy and appreciate.

Why is the Qur'an in Arabic?

When I had to learn Arabic with the teacher, I would get home and think: *I wish the Qur'an was in English or Turkish! I would read it so well that way.*

But, if the letters of the Qur'an were in English, I probably wouldn't have read it anyway. I was lazy and this thought was only an excuse to ease my guilt.

But it did make me think: *Why is the Qur'an in Arabic?*

The answer to this question isn't that hard to explain.

The Prophet Muhammad (peace be upon him) was an Arab and he lived in Arabia, amongst Arabs.

So, it shouldn't be a surprise that the Qur'an is in Arabic. Otherwise, the Prophet and those around him wouldn't have understood it. A Turkish, French or Chinese Qur'an wasn't going to be sent to an Arabic prophet, who lived amongst people that only understood Arabic.

Would Allah, He who knows everything, who fills the heavens and the earth, do such an unwise thing?

Of course not!

It does lead us to another question: *Why was the Prophet Muhammad chosen from amongst the Arabs? Why wasn't the final prophet from another race?*

Now, before answering this question, let's imagine we are Chinese Muslims. In that case we would say: "Why wasn't the Prophet chosen from amongst the Chinese? Then the Qur'an would be in Chinese!"

If we are English Muslims, what would we say? "Why wasn't the Prophet chosen from amongst the English? If that had been the case, the Qur'an would be in English!"

You see, there's no end to this! These types of questions could be asked for all races and languages on Earth.

Changing the nationality of the prophet or the language of the Qur'an doesn't help. The problem doesn't go away. Some people would always be left upset.

Allah had to do what was wisest. He chose a continent from all the continents, a country from all the countries, a language from all the languages and picked a prophet, from all the people, to send the Qur'an to.

Just like when He was creating the universe, He chose blue for the sky and green for the forests…

Just like He chose to give wings to birds and trunks to elephants…

Just like He chose to give hardness to rocks, freshness to water…

Just as we don't think to say, "Birds should have trunks", we also have no need to say, "Those elephants should fly": because that is the way they have been created.

Just as Allah chooses what should fly, what should swim and the animals that can run, He chooses His Messenger from whatever race He wants and sends His book in whatever language He wants.

So we shouldn't say, "The Qur'an should have been in Turkish, or such and such a language...", and we shouldn't say, "The Prophet should have been Turkish or from such and such a race rather than Arabic..."

Allah creates everything with wisdom and in the most beautiful way. And who knows what wisdom there is in it.

Why should I read the Qur'an in Arabic?

BEFORE WE START, let's remember that the Qur'an was first revealed in Arabic. When you see it in English, or German, or Chinese, it is a translation. A person has changed the words from Arabic into another language.

Although a translation might have the same cover, and it might be called the Qur'an, there is a big difference. Can you guess it?

The Arabic words were chosen by Allah – the creator of the universe. The Qur'an is Allah's word.

In a translation, a person has had to choose the words. However good they are, however nice they sound the words are different.

Of course, the person that translated it has made sure it has the same meaning, but nevertheless, it is not the same as before.

Think about your reflection in the mirror. Is it the same as you? Definitely not. It looks just like you, but only on the surface. It doesn't have your heart or soul.

Even when it comes to the books that people write, translations are never as good as the original.

There are even some people who go and learn another language simply to read an author in their original language. For example, many people learn English to be able to read the works of William Shakespeare, French to read Victor Hugo and German to read Goethe.

So it shouldn't surprise you to hear that people all over the world are learning to read Arabic right now.

They want to read Allah's words exactly as He revealed them.

What a treat it is to read the Qur'an in its original language.

If a translation of the Qur'an isn't the same, should I read it?

Of course you should. It will help you understand it.

A translation of the Qur'an gives you a glimpse of the meaning. And the meaning is very important.

Wherever you are living in the world, whatever language you are speaking, every Muslim should read the meaning.

Allah says in the Qur'an:

This is a message to all people, so that they may be warned by it, and know that He is the only God, and so that those who have minds may take heed.

Surah Ibrahim 14:52

The Qur'an is neither a book just for Arabs, nor has it been sent just for those who know how to read Arabic. It's a book for all humankind. Just like the Prophet is the prophet for all humankind.

In that case, all the people on Earth should read it and try to understand it.

But, to do so, everyone would have to learn Arabic, or the Qur'an would need to be translated into every language.

It's impossible for everyone to learn Arabic, so it's best to translate the Qur'an into all of the languages of the world.

Today there are translations of the Qur'an in nearly every language that is being used on Earth. Whether they are Muslim or not, everyone can read the Qur'an's meaning in a translation.

Is reading the meaning (the translation of the Qur'an) enough for us?

Let's use our imagination. Picture this. There is a spectacular palace full of countless treasures and priceless art in front of you.

The door of this palace is remarkable. Its walls are covered in beautiful colours and patterns.

But, the beauty of the door and the outside is nothing compared to the beauty of the palace inside.

You want to go inside, don't you? Just seeing the outside is nice, but the inside will take your breath away.

Now, a translation of the Qur'an is like this. It shows you what is on the outside; it gives you a glimpse of its beauty.

However, to see the palace's treasures more closely, you have to get inside and spend time there.

It is the same with the Qur'an. The really marvellous things are on the inside.

Just reading the words, without trying to understand what they mean, is good, but it isn't enough for an inquisitive little child like you.

Now, how about I offer you a guide to the palace? One that tells you how to get inside and where to find the treasures!

Well, there are thousands of guides to the Qur'an to choose from.

Over the centuries, many great teachers have written books to help us, explaining the wonders inside the Qur'an.

These explanations are like guidebooks. They take us around the Qur'an verse by verse, giving us help and guidance. We call them *tafsirs*.

Tafsirs give us a much deeper understanding of the Qur'an.

An understanding that will show us the priceless antiques and the countless treasures that we might have missed before.

Let me give you another example.

Reading the Qur'an but not understanding it is like only seeing the surface of the sea. We look at it, gaze at its vast blueness and the shimmery movements under the sun, and think it is a beautiful. But we know the sea is so much more.

With its millions of fish, pearls and corals, the sea is magical kingdom. Far different and much more beautiful than it can be seen from the surface.

Like the sea, the Qur'an is full of wonders. Just imagine what treasures are inside the book of Allah.

Should I read the Qur'an in Arabic if I don't understand it?

People, a teaching from your Lord has come to you, a healing for what is in [your] hearts, and guidance and mercy for the believers.

Surah Yunus 10:57

AS MUSLIMS, HOWEVER much we thank God it is not enough, because we have the joy to read and listen to the Qur'an in the language it was revealed in.

All of the other books that were sent to earlier prophets either do not exist or the words have been changed.

But not the Qur'an.

In a cave near Makkah, 1,400 years ago, the Angel Gabriel brought the Prophet the first verse:

Read! In the Name of your Lord Who created.
Surah al-'Alaq 96:1

Today, all Muslims on Earth, whatever language they speak can, with a bit of effort, learn to read this verse in Arabic.

This is the case for the first verse revealed, and all the way to the last verse revealed.

Just think how special that is. We are using the same words that the Prophet taught his companions, that Angel Gabriel taught the Prophet, that Allah told to Angel Gabriel.

This is a great blessing that fills my heart with joy.

The language of the Quran: Islam's common language

Wherever they're from, whatever language they speak, Muslims all recite the Qur'an in Arabic when they pray.

It doesn't matter whether the person is Chinese, Arabic, Turkish or English; they have to read the first verse in the Qur'an, *al-Fatihah*, and a few other verses during the prayer.

This is the minimum Muslims should try to learn. This isn't a very hard thing to do. Memorising the surahs to perform *salah* (prayer), and learning how to perform *salah*, is just as easy as memorising the times tables.

Allah revealed some short surahs in the last chapter of the Qur'an, such as Surah *al-Ikhlas* (Purity), Surah *al-Kawthar* (Abundance), Surah *al-Fil* (The Elephant). Not all surahs are long, like *al-Baqarah*. These short surahs are usually read in less than a minute!

To this day, I've never seen anyone who performs *salah* complain about reading the surahs in Arabic!

Once you know some surahs off by heart you should learn what the words mean, especially Surah *al-Fatiha*.

Reading the Qur'an is rewarding

Reading the Qur'an is a rewarding act. The Prophet said that for every letter of the Qur'an a person reads, a reward is written for the reader. During the month of Ramadan, and in particular when it is *Laylat al-Qadr*, the night of power, these rewards are multiplied many times.

By the way, listening to the Qur'an being read is also just like reading it.

The Prophet had many hadiths on this topic. He often recommended his companions to read the Qur'an and think about the Qur'an.

The Prophet said: *"The most superior among you [Muslims] are those who learn the Qur'an and teach it."*

al-Bukhari

Allah's Messenger said: *"The example of the person who knows the Qur'an by heart is like the owner of tied camels. If he keeps them tied, he will control them, but if he releases them, they will run away."*

al-Bukhari

The Prophet said: *"Keep on reciting the Qur'an, for, by Him in Whose Hand my life is, Qur'an runs away [is forgotten] faster than camels that are released from their tying ropes."*

al-Bukhari

The Prophet said: *"The example of him [a believer] who recites the Qur'an is like that of a citron which tastes good and smells good. And he [a believer] who does not recite the Qur'an is like a date which is good in taste but has no smell."*

al-Bukhari

The Messenger said: *"The one who is proficient in the recitation of the Qur'an will be with the honourable and obedient angels and he who recites the Qur'an and finds it difficult to recite, doing his best to recite it in the best way possible, will have a double reward."*

Muslim

Why did Allah use words in the Qur'an?

We have made it easy, in your own language [Prophet], so that you may bring glad news to the righteous and warnings to a stubborn people.

Surah Maryam 19:97

ALLAH IS SPEAKING to us in the Qur'an. The words we read are the ones He chose to use. But that makes me think of a question: *Why does Allah use words that are familiar to us? Couldn't He have chosen to speak to us in another way?*

I mean, Allah was there when nothing was. He does not need anything. He can do anything.

So, why is the book of Allah so familiar to us? Allah isn't like anything He created, so shouldn't His word be completely different too? Why would he use the words of people?

A book for humanity

As our eyes can't see every colour, our ears can't hear every sound. Even if our ears could hear everything, our mind would not understand what it all meant.

We can't hear bees speaking to one another very well. And we can't understand what they say.

When birds call to each other, it sounds to us like a beautiful song. We don't understand what birds say to each other, we only hear the sounds.

Even if you forget about these examples, remember this: we can't even understand another human when they speak a different language.

Our ears have been created in a particular way. We only hear some noises. And our hearts and minds only understand things that are familiar to us.

If Allah didn't speak in a way we could understand; if He addressed us in a language that's appropriate to Allah's might, His glory, we wouldn't know what was being said to us.

For us to understand, either we would need to be raised up to a new level, one where we could be spoken to in Allah's language, or Allah, from His compassion and mercy, would need to address us in a language, in a way, that we know.

Allah chose to address us in an understandable language. Just like when a mother is talking to her baby, she chooses an understandable language.

Have you ever seen a mother talking to her small child?

Even if she was the world's most brilliant scientist, a mother will talk to her child in a way the child can understand. She will leave

all her knowledge, all the words she knows, on one side to communicate with her dear child.

She'll say: "Look, open your mouth! Ahhhhh. Here comes the food!" She'll tickle her child during play and say: "Coochie coochie coo."

Someone who heard this, but didn't see the mother and child, would not accept that the mother is so clever. They might say: "This cannot be the world's most brilliant scientist."

This is an example to those who say after reading the Qur'an: "The Qur'an uses words. It sounds similar to our own. If the Qur'an was Allah's word, it wouldn't be like ours. It should be a miraculous thing!"

They don't understand that Allah is speaking to them in an understandable language for their own good.

Just like the people that say: "Why does the Prophet Muhammad get hungry, get cold, get tired. Shouldn't a prophet be like an angel?"

Who can follow in the footsteps of an angel who doesn't eat, drink or get hungry? Their life wouldn't be an example for us to follow.

Just like prophets were sent to be a guide for people, the Qur'an is for humans.

It's for people to understand, get advice from and live according to what they have learned.

This is a message to all people, so that they may be warned by it, and know that He is the only God, and so that those who have minds may take heed.

Surah Ibrahim 14:52

Yes, the Qur'an sounds familiar to us, because it is meant to be understood.

What is the point of Allah sending us a book if we could not learn from it? A book that no one could read, or no one could bear to listen to, wouldn't be of any use to us.

We should thank Allah, who sent a book that we can read and understand. A book that guides us, that gives us knowledge that will help us lead good lives and take us away from harm.

The Qur'an: A unique book

A question such as this may come to you. *Since the Qur'an has been sent in a language humans can understand, why is it unique and without equal? Why is it a miracle? Isn't it like other books?*

I can see why you might ask that. Let me start by saying this:

What do we make out of earth?

We make pots, vases, dishes and mugs.

What does Allah make out of earth?

He makes fruit, trees, vegetables…

He makes a rose bush, an olive tree and a plump potato…

He makes a bird, a sheep and even humans from earth…

He even makes the earth.

Can you see the enormous difference between Allah's skill and our own? What he can do is impossible for us.

Now let's think about words.

Writers have written stories, poems and

songs for thousands of years.

With the same words Allah revealed the Qur'an to the Prophet. No other book is like it.

It soothes people's minds.

When recited out loud it lifts sad hearts.

It tells us to think about the world. It even includes scientific facts that were unknown when the Qur'an was revealed.

It guides us in this life and teaches us about the next life.

Its message has reached billions of people.

Nothing written before or after it was revealed can compare to it.

What a good companion the Qur'an is. It is like a sun that brightens our lives.

Alif Lam Mim Ra. These are the signs of the Book. What your Lord has sent down to you [Prophet] is the truth, yet most people do not believe.

Surah al-Ra'd 13:1

51

Why was the Qur'an revealed over such a long time?

*And it is a recitation that We have revealed
in parts, so that you can recite it to people at
intervals; We have sent it down little by little.*
Surah al-Isra 17:106

JUST AS EVERYTHING in the universe was created bit by bit, the Qur'an was revealed verse by verse.

The Qur'an was given to the Prophet Muhammad over 23 years. He was 40 years old when he received the first verse from the Angel Gabriel. The rest came in stages over his life as a messenger.

But why wasn't it revealed all at once?

To understand that, we need to imagine ourselves in Makkah, the place where the first verse of the Qur'an was sent to the Prophet Muhammad.

In Makkah, the people did not have good habits. In fact, some were evil.

They drank alcohol and gambled. All they were interested in was making money. And they would not share it with the poor or help the needy. Worst of all, they buried their newborn daughters in the desert.

The Makkans made idols and worshipped them. They asked them for help and success when they themselves had made them.

A book that told them all of this was wrong would not have been a joy to read.

Following the message of the Qur'an would have meant giving up their bad habits all at once.

That would not have been easy.

And it would have made the Prophet Muhammad's job much harder.

He would have to memorise the entire Qur'an, at once.

He would have had to ask people to change their whole lives.

Imagine one morning having to change everything you believed.

Following Allah's rules would have been very hard for the Makkan people.

They might have stopped trying to follow the new rules or, worse still, turned their backs on the Qur'an altogether.

Change takes time

Instead, the verses of the Qur'an came bit by bit. Over a long time.

The people of Makkah, and Arabia, could learn each verse off by heart, think about what it meant, and then change their ways.

It was not just given to them like a list of instructions.

Both their minds and hearts were being changed as they learned and absorbed Allah's verses.

Instead of having to alter their ways all at once, the people only had to make small changes. What a relief that must have been to them, and a great mercy from Allah.

This way everything they learned stayed with them.

It never left their hearts and minds.

If Allah had wished, of course He could have sent the Qur'an all at once. He created the universe and everything in it. Nothing is too hard for Him.

But, had He sent it all together, the people would have faced great difficulty.

They would have had to remember it all by heart, and try to understand what it all meant.

It would have been like a child, who can barely read, being sent to university. Can you imagine that? They would be sent straight home, without learning a thing.

During the time of the Prophet, those who hated the Prophet and the Qur'an said things like: "Why would Allah send His book line by line? He should send it all at once."

The answer to their question was given to them in a verse of the Qur'an:

The disbelievers also say, 'Why was the Qur'an not sent down to him all at once?' We sent it in this way to strengthen your heart [Prophet]; We gave it to you in gradual revelation.

Surah al-Furqan 25:32

Other books were also sent before the Qur'an. The Torah was sent to Prophet Moses. The *Injeel* was sent to Prophet Jesus. But the Qur'an was the last book sent to humankind. So it had to be understood very well and the people had to follow its rules. After all it had to be passed on to people all around the world, until the Day of Judgement.

At the start of the revelations, the people of Makkah were like stones – on the ground and covered in dirt. Due to the lessons they learned from the Qur'an, they were slowly transformed. Twenty-three years later, they were like the stars that shine in the sky.

Their light is still guiding us today.

How do we know that the Qur'an has not been changed?

We have sent down the Qur'an Ourself, and We Ourself will guard it. Even before you [Prophet]
Surah al-Hijr 15:9

NOT ONLY MUSLIMS, but many other people, believe the Qur'an has not been changed! People of other religions, people of no religion and even history teachers.

It doesn't matter that the Qur'an was sent 1,400 years ago. It is still the same. It has never changed: not even one chapter, one verse or even one letter.

Isn't that an amazing fact?

And a fact many people believe. Even if they are not Muslim.

Some people who don't accept that Muhammad is a prophet, have a deep respect for his life. And there are people who look at the history of the Qur'an and believe it is exactly the same, despite how many years ago it was written.

How has the Qur'an been sent to us?

Angel Gabriel brought Allah's verses to the Prophet. Sometimes the Prophet was able to see the Angel Gabriel. Sometimes he wasn't.

The Prophet would sweat and go pale when the verses were given to him. It could even sound like the ringing of a bell in his head.

Once the Prophet received the verses he instantly memorised them. In fact, he was so careful not to forget them, he repeated the verses many times.

63

Then Allah sent him a verse that removed his fears, and assured him that Allah protected the Qur'an:

[Prophet], do not rush your tongue in an attempt to hasten [your memorization of] the Revelation.

Surah al-Qiyamah 75:16-17

Scribes and hafiz (memorisers of the Qur'an)

The Prophet had many companions that spent as much time as possible with him: observing him; asking him questions; and helping him on his mission.

Some of them knew how to read and write. At first, there were only a few but, in time, their number rose to as many as 40. They were called SCRIBES.

Each scribe had a special place among the companions. Their most important duty was

to write the verses down that came to the
Prophet.

As the Prophet didn't know how to read
and write, he couldn't do it himself. Instead,
his companions did so, as soon as a verse was
revealed. This would be good enough for most
people, but not the scribes. They would read
what they had written to the Prophet to check
it was exactly right.

Along with the verses, Gabriel told the
Prophet what the order of the verses should be.
This was also recorded.

You might wonder, *where did they get paper from to write it down?* That is an excellent question.

They didn't have any paper.

In that time, the Arabs did not read or write. Instead, everything was remembered and passed from generation to generation by talking.

You might also wonder how this was possible. Well, their memories were very good. In fact, there were some Arabs who could play chess while travelling on a camel, without a board or pieces, just from their imagination. Of course, for a community that had such strong memories, it wasn't very hard to memorise the verses of the Qur'an.

However, despite their amazing memories, it was still important to write down vital information. They could do this on flat stone slabs, animal skins and date leaves.

As well as scribes, there were also HAFIZ, people who would memorise the Qur'an.

The tradition of memorising the Qur'an is a custom that continues today.

Hafiz of the Qur'an learn the verses one by one and repeat them often. At the time of the Prophet, there were more hafiz than scribes. Everybody had a good memory, but not many people could read or write.

And, as you read in the previous chapter, the verses were revealed piece by piece. This made it easier to memorise them.

During the Prophet's lifetime, the written verses were not brought together to form a book, because the revelations continued. And the verses did not come in the order we read them today.

So, it wasn't known beforehand what the final order would be. If it had been turned into a book, before it was complete, everything would change; a new version would have to be written.

The Qur'an (Mushaf)

When the Prophet passed away, his loyal friend, Abu Bakr, became the head of the Muslim community.

During Abu Bakr's leadership there were many battles. Lots of Muslims were killed, including the hafiz – the trustworthy people who had memorised the Qur'an.

This situation worried Umar, who would later become a leader of the Muslims. He feared that if hafiz continued to die, there wouldn't be anyone left who knew the Qur'an off by heart!

Umar shared this worry with Abu Bakr.

Therefore, it was decided that the Qur'an should be turned into a book.

Zayd b. Thabit, who was both a hafiz and a scribe, was asked to do this job.

He was helped by a team made up of Umar, Ali, Uthman and Ubayy Ibn Ka'ab.

They all carried out the work for exactly one year.

Although Zayd b. Thabit knew the Qur'an from memory, he didn't sit and write the verses on his own.

He called upon anyone that had learned something of the Qur'an from Allah's Messenger to bring it to him.

Anyone who had written a verse brought it to him. And those who had it in memory came and read it to him. Zayd compared the verses that were brought to him and read to him. In the end, all the verses were written on skins and date leaves and put into the same order as it is today.

Once complete, it was read from start to finish twice.

The Qur'an had become a book. It was called MUSHAF (Qur'an).

During the time of Uthman, Islam's third leader after the Prophet, this book was copied and sent to all the cities of the Islamic empire.

Today, in many Muslim countries, there are very old copies of the Qur'an. For example, in a museum in Istanbul, there are Qur'ans that belonged to Uthman and Ali.

There isn't the slightest difference between them and the Qur'ans that are being read today.

The Qur'an was protected and preserved from the time of the Prophet until today. It has stayed the same, thanks to the people that remembered it and wrote it down.

That is how we know a letter has not been changed.

And it will not be changed until the Day of Judgement, because Allah is protecting it.

We have sent down the Qur'an Ourself, and We Ourself will guard it. Even before you [Prophet].

Surah al-Hijr 15:9

Science in the Qur'an

ALLAH MENTIONS THE universe in the Qur'an a lot. But why?

Because He wants us to think, look and reflect on the world around us. He talks about animals, plants, mountains and much more.

When reading the Qur'an we think about the universe; and when examining the universe we should think of the Qur'an.

For example, read this verse from the Qur'an:

And your Lord inspired the bee, saying, "Build yourselves houses in the mountains and trees and what people construct..."

Surah Al-Nahl 16:68

It makes you think of bees flying in front of our eyes.

Whenever we decide to eat a spoon full of honey another verse about honey bees should come to mind:

From their bellies comes a drink of different colours in which there is healing for people. There truly is a sign in this for those who think.

Surah Al-Nahl 16:69

Can you see that the Qur'an and the universe are two books of Allah that should never be separated from each other?

The Qur'an's verses tell us about the miracles of the universe. They inform us about stars, clouds, thunder, bees, ants and even our adventures in our mother's womb.

And as we learn the secrets of nature we understand the verses of the Qur'an better.

For example, scientists studying bees have discovered that honey starts off as a 'drink' from the bellies of bees, and about all the goodness of honey for humans.

Scientists looking at the planets in the universe discovered they follow orbits. Well, listen to what the Qur'an said 1400 years ago about this:

It is He who created night and day, the sun and the moon, each floating in its orbit.
Surah Al-Anbiyaa 21:33

This is one of the greatest miracles of the Qur'an. It shows that as time passes the Qur'an doesn't get old; as a matter of fact it gets younger.

Is the Qur'an a book of science?

When the Qur'an talks about the world it isn't to explain scientific facts. It is to draw your attention to Allah's wonderful workmanship.

If it mentions the stars, it mentions them to show Allah's might.

If it mentions honeybees, it mentions them so we can see the complexity of Allah's creation.

This is because the Qur'an is a holy book first. Its main purpose is to introduce us to Allah and inform us of Him.

It orders us to think, to look and to reflect on the universe to understand Allah and His Qur'an!

"There truly is a sign in this for those who think."

Surah Al-Nahl 16:69

The Qur'an doesn't say, "This is how these things happen…" like a biology book, a chemistry book or a geography book.

The Qur'an tells us to think and to look at the world for ourselves.

For this reason, reading the Qur'an will not make you a biologist, a chemist or a geologist. To be one of those you have to carry out experiments, conduct research and make observations about the world.

Many great Muslim scientists of the past were inspired to do just that.

Do you wonder what they achieved?

Great Muslim Scientists

Hundreds of years ago cities all over the Muslim world were full of great scientists.

They were scientists who read the Qur'an and studied the universe. For centuries their discoveries amazed people.

They said, "Doesn't the Qur'an order us to look, think and reflect on His creation? Since there are so many verses about the universe in the Qur'an shouldn't we look at them side by side?"

Let's learn about a few of these amazing people.

'Abbas ibn Firnas (810–887): More than 1000 years ago, he made an early parachute jump and leaped off the Great Mosque of Cordoba, Spain, wearing a reinforced cloak.

Al-Battani (858–929): He was one of the most influential figures in trigonometry, a branch of maths. He is considered to be one of the greatest Muslim astronomers and mathematicians.

Al-Biruni (973–1052): He discussed the theory of the Earth rotating around its own axis, 600 years before a scientist called Galileo talked about it in Europe.

Al-Idrisi (1100–1166): In 1154, he finished the first map that showed most of North Africa, Asia, and Europe.

Al-Khwarizmi (780–850): He is the father of algebra, a type of mathematics that uses letters and numbers.

Fatima al-Fihri (d. 880): She used her fortune to build the Al-Qarawiyyin mosque and a school in Morocco 1,200 years ago. This is the world's oldest active university.

Ibn al-Haytham (965–1040): He revolutionised optics, the science of light and sight. He was the first to prove that vision is caused by light reflecting off an object and entering the eye.

Ibn Sina (980–1037): As a doctor and philosopher, he developed a method of treating fractured bones that is still used today. He is considered the father of modern medicine.

Jabir ibn Hayyan (721–815): He was known in the west as Geber, and he is the founder of chemistry. All his experiments were carried out in his laboratory in Kufa, which is now in Iraq.

Al-Jahiz (779–869): He was a pioneer in zoology and wrote a seven-volume *Book of Animals*, which had observations on ants, communication between animals and food chains.

Al-Zahrawi (936–1013): This Spanish Muslim surgeon is considered the father of modern surgery. He produced many of the medical instruments that continue to be used, like the scalpel for cutting.

Look what kind of fruits grow when the Qur'an and the universe are read together at the same time!

Why does it say: "Will they not then consider the camels... ?" in the Qur'an?

Will they not then consider the camels, how they are created?

Surah al-Ghashiyah 88:17

THE QUR'AN IS full of meaning. Allah has sent it down to guide us to what is right and away from what is wrong.

However, sometimes it isn't clear what the Qur'an is telling us straight away.

If you are like me, then you wonder about those verses in the Qur'an you don't understand. I wondered why the Qur'an asks: "Will they not then consider the camels"?

Before we look at this verse, let us first think about the people who first heard it. They were Arabs from Makkah and Madinah. And camels were essential for them. So the Arabs would have been thinking about camels every day, even if you aren't where you live.

So, why then in the Qur'an is it asked: "Will they not then consider the camels"?

The Arabs at the time of the Prophet did consider camels. They rode them, ate the meat of them, drank the milk from them, used their skin for leather and made them carry their loads.

However, camels didn't remind the people of their Creator. They didn't think of Allah, who created such an amazing animal: an animal that can survive in a dry desert with hardly anything to drink.

They didn't thank Him for this great blessing. Instead, they took their camels for granted.

After riding them through the desert, they would dismount them and go to kneel before idols made out of stone and wood. Some would even sacrifice their camels to the idols.

They used camels every day, but didn't consider their beautiful and amazing Creator. This might have been because they didn't know Allah or because they didn't accept that the camel had been created by Allah.

Yet the verse wants us to think about this: "Will they not then consider the camels, how they are created?"

Considering the camels means thinking about how they were created and remembering who created them.

The Prophet was the guide for all Muslims. When it comes to understanding the Qur'an, his actions are very helpful.

One day a companion asked Aisha, a wife of the Prophet, about the manners of the Prophet.

She replied: "Have you not read the Qur'an? The morals of the Prophet are the same."

He was like a living Qur'an.

I wondered how the Prophet considered the camels. After flicking through a few books, I found a prayer the Prophet made when mounting a camel:

"Glory be to Him who has given us control over this; we could not have done it by ourselves".
Surah al-Zukhruf 43:13

So, this is how you can consider a camel in the way the Qur'an wants. If only there was a camel, so we could say it...

What can we learn from this verse?

Today, we don't travel on camels.

Most of us haven't even seen a real camel. So what does this verse mean for us? And how can we use the Prophet's prayer?

Well, even if we are not travelling on camels, we can get in cars, planes, trains and ships to travel around.

All of these things are blessings from Allah. We can get in these vehicles and travel over land, sea and through the air. They are made using the materials that Allah created. What's more, we fill them up with fuel that has been created by Allah. So, we should be thankful to Allah for them.

The prayer the Prophet made when getting on a camel can easily be said when getting in these vehicles.

"Glory be to Him who has given us control over this; we could not have done it by ourselves".
Surah al-Zukhruf 43:13

We need to remember that the Qur'an doesn't just want us to consider a camel and how it was created. It also wants us to consider how the skies were raised up, how mountains were fixed, how the earth spread and much more.

So let's remember Allah who filled our world with beauty and thank Him.

Why is the name of the longest surah in the Qur'an *al-Baqarah* (the cow)?

Remember when Moses said to his people, "God commands you to sacrifice a cow." They said, "Are you making fun of us?" He answered, "God forbid that I should be so ignorant."

Surah al-Baqarah 2:67

BAQARAH MEANS COW in Arabic. And yes, the name of the longest surah in the Qur'an is *al-Baqarah* (the cow).

But don't look for Surah *The Cow* because you probably won't find it. In a translation of the Qur'an, the surah names are not translated. They are like the names of people (proper nouns).

If your parents name you Yasser, it does not change when you visit another country. Even though Yasser means 'to be well off' in English, no one would start calling you 'to be well off' in England!

You will also not find Surah *al-'Ankabut* written as 'The Spider'; or Surah *al-Nahl* as 'The Bee'. And 'The Star' isn't written instead of Surah *al-Najm* and 'The Moon' instead of *al-Qamar*.

Another reason is because none of these surahs only talk of a spider, a bee, a star or the moon.

They take these 'special' names because of parts in each surah that cover these subjects.

The longest surah of the Qur'an, *al-Baqarah*, doesn't speak just of the cow. It covers so many subjects. We would need another book just to list *some* of them.

Yet Surah *al-Baqarah* does inform us of the 'cow incident', from verse 67 to verse 71.

What is so special about this cow incident that a surah has been named after it?

Well, a lot actually. It talks about a cow being killed, but there is so much more to it.

Slaughtering the cow

We need to go back to the Prophet Moses' time.

One night, a rich man living amongst the Sons of Israel was killed by his own nephew. But no one knew who the murderer was.

The next day, a group of people gathered around the man who had died. And that wicked nephew started shouting and said he wanted revenge.

They asked the Prophet Moses to tell them what to do.

Prophet Moses said to them: "God commands you to sacrifice a cow."

The Sons of Israel were surprised. They asked: "Are you making fun of us?"

Prophet Moses wasn't joking.

He said: "God forbid that I should be so ignorant."

What shocked and scared the Sons of Israel wasn't that Allah wanted them to kill a cow to find out who the murderer was. What was hard for them was to slaughter the cow.

Because, before the murder, when Prophet Moses had left for a short time to visit Mount Tur in Egypt, they had started worshipping

cows. Just like they had before, when the Sons of Israel were living in the country of Egypt.

In Egypt they worked on the land like everyone else.

Cows and cattle were essential for them.

Cows would plough their fields and carry their crops.

The people were very grateful to cows.

Over time, this gratitude turned into something else. Cows became holy animals.

They declared them as gods and started worshipping them.

The Sons of Israel, who had fled the Pharaoh with Prophet Moses, faced hardship in the desert and started to miss their time in Egypt.

They craved the old ways, and the things they had: jobs, land and cows.

During this time, Prophet Moses went to Mount Tur in Egypt for some time, leaving them alone.

When he left, a man called Samiri took advantage. He made a golden sculpture of a calf. This sculpture also mooed like a cow.

The people of Israel immediately gathered around the cow sculpture Samiri had made. And, after some time, they started to worship it.

When Prophet Moses came back from Mount Tur, he couldn't believe it. He had explained the oneness of Allah to them for years!

At this point, Allah ordered them to slaughter a cow.

They couldn't immediately find a cow to slaughter. They couldn't bring themselves to do it. After all, cows were special to them.

They started asking Prophet Moses what kind of a cow it had to be, secretly hoping to delay what had to be done.

They said, "Call on your Lord for us, to show us what sort of cow it should be." He answered, "God says it should be neither too old nor too young, but in between, so do as you are commanded."

They said, "Call on your Lord for us, to show us what colour it should be." He answered, "God says it should be a bright yellow cow, pleasing to the eye."

They said, "Call on your Lord for us, to show us [exactly] what it is: all cows are more or less alike to us. With God's will, we shall be guided."

He replied, "It is a perfect and unblemished cow, not trained to till the earth or water the fields." They said, "Now you have brought the truth," and so they slaughtered it, though they almost failed to do so.

Surah al-Baqarah 2:68–71

In the end, they did it. They slaughtered a cow, though "they almost failed to do so."

Then, Allah ordered them to hit the dead body of the person who had been murdered with part of the slaughtered cow's meat. Once they did this, a miracle occurred. The dead person came to life and told the people who the murderer was.

Worship Allah alone

The people in the story had stopped believing in Allah and started worshiping a cow.

It might not cross your mind to worship cows. But a cow is a symbol. Everything that comes between Allah and you is actually a holy cow.

We all have one or more cows we need to give up.

And, unless we give them up, they will remain between us and Allah and continue to moo.

For example, television that kills time is a cow for most of us. It stays between us and Allah.

We miss *salah* times and ignore our jobs; sitting there lazily when we could be helping our parents or playing with friends.

If we spend most of our time in front of the TV, it just keeps on mooing.

We don't have time to read the Qur'an and busy ourselves with useful books.

In this way, the TV will remain in front of us like Samiri's mooing cow.

Once in a while, we should 'cut' it out of our lives.

And we shouldn't make up excuses to keep bad things like the Sons of Israel did.

Now, try and count the cows you see around you.

See how the cow in Surah *al-Baqarah* came and found its place in our lives.

The name of the longest surah of the Qur'an is full of wisdom. I hope now you can see it.

The Dictionary
of the Qur'an

QUR'AN: The Muslim holy book. Sent to humanity through the last Prophet, Muhammed.

As Muslims believe no other prophets will come, they also believe no other books will come either.

Not even one word in the Qur'an has been changed since the day it was sent.

The Qur'an has other names too. In the Qur'an, Allah calls it *Kitab* "Book". *Furqan* is another one of the Qur'an's names. It means the one that separated truth from lies, right from wrong, unlawful (haram) from lawful (halal), good from bad. Another name for the Qur'an is *Shifa*, because it heals hearts. And *Hakim* (Wise) is another one of the Qur'an's well-known names. Sometimes the Qur'an is called *Qur'an-i Hakim*. Hakim means wise and the source of wisdom.

MUSHAF: This means pages gathered between two covers. It is another name of the Qur'an.

REVELATION: Knowledge sent from Allah. Normally shared with prophets by the Angel Gabriel (the angel of revelation).

GABRIEL: There are four great angels: Michael, Israfel, Malak al-Mawt (Angel of Death) and Gabriel. These four great angels have different duties. Gabriel is the ANGEL OF REVELATION, whose job is to take revelations from Allah to a prophet.

SURAH: The Qur'an is made up of 114 chapters. These chapters are called surahs. All of the surahs, except one, start with the Basmala – In the name of Allah, the Lord of Mercy, the Giver of Mercy.

Each surah has a different name. These names are to do with the topics that are mentioned in them.

For example, one surah is called *al-Ankabut*. *Al-Ankabut* means 'the spider'. In this surah there is a verse about a spider. And Surah Yusuf takes its name from the verses in the chapter that refer to the Prophet Yusuf.

The most well-known surah is *al-Fatihah*. This is the first surah of the Qur'an and is the most often read part of the Qur'an. Muslims cannot pray without reading *al-Fatihah* at least twice.

The longest surah is *al-Baqarah*, which has 286 verses. The shortest one is *al-Kawthar* (The Heavenly Fount). It has three verses.

VERSE: Surahs (chapters) are made up of verses. A verse is like a sentence of the Qur'an. Some sentences are long, some are very short. The Qur'an was revealed verse by verse over 23 years. In the first 13 years, the Prophet was in Madinah; the other 10 years were spent in Madinah. Verses sent to the Prophet in Makkah are called Makki, and verses sent in Madinah are called Madani.

JUZ (CHAPTER): The Qur'an is split into 30 parts, or Juz. Many Muslims read the Qur'an part by part.

HAFIZ (MEMORISER OF THE QURAN): People who know the Qur'an off by heart are called hafiz. The profession of being a hafiz has existed since the Prophet's times. The companions memorised every verse that was revealed. And they taught the verses to students, and so on, until thousands of people had memorised the Qur'an.

KHATM (COMPLETING THE RECITATION OF THE QUR'AN): Reciting the Qur'an from start to finish is called a khatm. This is a sunnah of the Prophet, an action he performed. Every year, especially during the month of Ramadan, he read all the verses of the Qur'an with the Angel Gabriel.

When all of the Qur'an had been revealed, they did this twice. They read the Qur'an to each other and listened to be sure that the Qur'an was completed and accurate. A short time after, the Prophet left the world, leaving two great items, his sunnah (actions and deeds) and the Qur'an itself.

Today, Muslims continue the tradition of completing the Qur'an, especially during the month of Ramadan.

MEANING (of the Qur'an): A translation of the Qur'an from Arabic, which is the original language, into another language is called the meaning. The meaning and the Qur'an are not the same things. So the translations cannot replace the Arabic Qur'an.

TAFSIR: Books that explain the verses of the Qur'an. During the history of Islam, thousands of volumes of *tafsirs* have been written.

About the author

ÖZKAN ÖZE WAS born in Turkey in 1974. While at high school, he started working at Zafer magazine's editorial office in Istanbul and discovered his love of literature and books. Since then he has gone on to become the editor of Zafer Publications Group and continually writes. He is married with two children.

Özkan wrote the "I Wonder About Islam" series because he believes that questions are prayers. Asking one is like saying, "Teach me to understand." They act as keys that lead us through doors to new worlds that are more interesting and beautiful than we thought possible.

The "I Wonder About Islam" series

The "I Wonder About Islam" series give young readers answers to the BIG questions they have about Islam in brilliant little books. Written in a friendly and accessible style for today's youth, they are essential companions for questioning young minds.

Books in the "I Wonder About Islam" series:

I Wonder About Allah (Book One)

I Wonder About Allah (Book Two)

I Wonder About the Prophet (Book Three)

I Wonder About the Qur'an (Book Four)